The Trailblazing
Mary O'Toole

Pioneering Woman on the Bench

By Nichola D. Gutgold & Paula M. Mulhall
Illustrated by Leigh O'Connell

Eifrig Publishing LLC

Berlin Lemont

Published by Eifrig Publishing,
PO Box 66, Lemont, PA 16851, USA
Knobelsdorffstr. 44, 14059 Berlin, Germany

For information regarding permission, write to:
Rights and Permissions Department,
Eifrig Publishing,
PO Box 66, Lemont, PA 16851, USA.
permissions@eifrigpublishing.com, +1-8149549445

Library of Congress Cataloging-in-Publication Data
Gutgold, Nichola D. & Paula M. Mulhall

A Judicial Trailblazer: Mary O'Toole, Pioneering Woman on the Bench /
 by Nichola D. Gutgold & Paula M. Mulhall, Illustrated by Leigh O'Connell

p. cm.

Paperback: ISBN 978-1-63233-351-3
Hard cover: ISBN 978-1-63233-352-0
eBook: ISBN 978-1-63233-353-7

[1. Biography/Women - Juvenile Non-Fiction. 2. U.S. Supreme Court - Juvenile Non-Fiction.]

I. Leigh O'Connell, ill. II. Title

27 26 25 24 23
5 4 3 2 1
Printed on recycled acid-free paper. ∞

Have you ever dreamed of living somewhere else?

Where would you go?

Mary O'Toole was born on April 4, 1874 to a large, loving family in *County Carlow, Ireland.*

Ireland is an island country in Europe, known for its rugged green landscape, shamrocks, castles, music, farming, and leprechauns.

As a girl, she worked alongside her parents and brothers and sisters in the fields of her family's small farm. Mary had eleven brothers and sisters!

In the evenings, her family would
gather around a warm fire.

Mary loved listening to family stories about
traveling to America. It sounded like a magical
place, and she dreamed of someday going there
on a big ship and starting a new life.

When Mary was 7 years old, she became aware
that her father was active in local justice
causes and heard stories about his meetings
during family conversations. Her dad, Nicholas,
wanted to make life better in their community,
and sometimes his beliefs got him in trouble.
Mary took all of this in, and it would influence
her choices later in life.

But Mary didn't just dream about changing her life by sailing to America, she made it happen, slowly but surely.

She took on small jobs, such as mending clothing and running errands for her neighbors. She saved every penny she earned.

At age 16, all of her hard work and saving paid off
when she left Ireland and sailed to America,
accompanied by her brother Mike, her aunt (her
mother's sister) and uncle on a ship named
SS Fulda, which was built in 1883.

When she arrived in the United States, she lived with her aunt and uncle in New York, but she missed her parents and her brothers and sisters.

She earned her keep by working as a nanny and taking care of children during the day, and in the evening she went to school to learn *stenography*. She kept busy, trying to make her life better by learning new things.

Because she was the top student in her class,
she was recommended by her business school
to take a position as a stenographer for
Judge Monroe Wheeler for $1,200 a year.

She began to take a keen interest
in the study of law.

Judge Wheeler noticed that Mary often read poetry in the evenings. Judge Wheeler encouraged Mary to read law books instead of *Shakespeare* or *Thomas Moore*, which she enjoyed, and that was the beginning of her law studies.

When Judge Wheeler retired, he presented her with the contents of his law library.

She moved to Washington, DC, and while working full time at the forestry department of the federal government, she also studied at the Washington College of Law. This was the first law school founded *by* women and explicitly *for* women (although men were also admitted), as it was still very difficult for women to get advanced education. She completed her *Master's Degree* in Laws in 1914.

Mary opened her own law office and became the first female *Municipal Court Judge* in the U.S..

Her seal of office had to have the word "his" crossed out in pen to be replaced with the word "hers".

President Harding appointed her to be the first Judge of the Municipal Court of Washington, D.C. in 1921. She was one of only three women judges in the United States at the time.

In January 1928, E. E. Dudding, national president of the Prisoner's Aid Society, wrote to the Department of Justice nominating O'Toole to fill the vacancy on the bench of the *District of Columbia* Supreme Court caused by the resignation of Judge Adolph Hoehling, stating:

"There is no better lawyer in Washington or anywhere else. She knows the law. She is judicial. She would make one of the best judges to be found and would, I think, raise public opinion of Federal courts."

Mary O'Toole became a well known judge in
Washington, DC and the very mention of her
name as a prospective member of the bench
made usually dignified men who had to appear
in court very nervous!

Did you know?

Mary O'Toole:

- was the first woman in the District of Columbia to perform a marriage ceremony.
- was the first woman director of the Washington, D.C. Chamber of Commerce
- did not believe in capital punishment (the death penalty)
- supported a woman's choice to divorce
- fought for women to have the right to vote

….these were very modern views, especially at the time!

Mary sailed from Ireland on July 21, 1891, and on the same day 30 years later, she became the first female municipal court judge in the U.S.!

WHAT DOES IT MEAN?

- **County Carlow, Ireland** is a county located in the South-East Region of Ireland, within the province of Leinster. Carlow is the second smallest and the third least populous of Ireland's 32 traditional counties.

- A **stenographer** is a person whose job is to transcribe speech in shorthand.

- **William Shakespeare** was an English playwright, poet and actor. He is widely regarded as the greatest writer in the English language and the world's greatest dramatist. He is often called England's national poet and the "Bard of Avon".

- **Thomas Moore** was a very popular Irish writer and poet, who also wrote lyrics to music.

- A **Master's Degree** is an academic degree awarded by universities or colleges upon completion of a course of study demonstrating mastery.

- A **Municipal Court Judge** is a judicial officer adjudicating traffic violations, certain minor liquor and drug violations, parking violations, city ordinances, code violations, and juvenile offenses to include: traffic, alcohol, vandalism, tobacco and any city ordinance.

- **District of Columbia** - Washington, DC, the U.S. capital, is a compact city on the Potomac River, bordering the states of Maryland and Virginia.

- **The Supreme Court** - As the final arbiter of the law, the Supreme Court is charged with ensuring the American people the promise of equal justice under the law and so it also functions as the guardian and interpreter of the Constitution.

- **The Washington Post** is an American daily newspaper published in Washington, D.C. It is the most-widely circulated newspaper within the Washington metropolitan area and has a large international audience.

Judge Mary O'Toole

16-year-old Mary O'Toole (MOT) set sail for the US from Ireland on July 21, 1891. Exactly 30 years later, on July 21, 1921, she was appointed as the first woman judge of a municipal court in the US.

Mary initially lived in Hornell, NY and worked as a nanny for a doctor while studying stenography in the evenings.

Mary moved to DC in 1905 and worked full time while attending the Washington College of Law. She graduated with her Bachelor of Law degree in 1908 and her Master's Degree in Laws in 1914.

Mary retired in 1936 due to ill health and she died in 1954. She is buried at Mount Olivet cemetery in a grave that was unmarked until recently. Mary's extended family had a grave marker placed on her final resting place in 2021 to correct this oversight, a fitting way to commemorate the centenary of her initial call to the bench.

About the Authors

Nichola D. Gutgold is a mother, a wife, a professor, a scholar-activist, and a proud steward of a Little Free Library! She holds a PhD in communication from Penn State. She is the author of a number of books about trailblazing women, including women who have run for the U.S. president, and this is her third scholarly book turned children's book to help young readers see all the potential for themselves. She enjoys engaging with the community with her books, and encourages everyone to speak up and speak well!

Paula M. Mulhall is a mother and proud "Ami" to two curious, adorable grandchildren. She grew up on a farm in Ireland with 10 siblings and moved to the US in her early 20's. She is a researcher, writer, poetry enthusiast, seeker and family-devotee. She is thrilled to be fulfilling a promise to her mother to research and recognize the life of Mary O'Toole (MOT), her Dad's aunt. "Mission MOT" started in January 2021 with the help of her wonderful extended O'Toole family around the world.

About the Illustrator

Leigh O'Connell is an Irish-based artist whose work takes inspiration from the local wildlife, history, faces and fabulous skies in North Clare on the Wild Atlantic Way. Her works are in various collections worldwide. Leigh's mother is from near to where Mary grew up. This is her first children's illustrated book.

Printed in Great Britain
by Amazon

22773136R10021